Tugboats

Contents

The Busy Port 2
At the Dock 6
Traveling on the River Road 10
Tugs: The Working Boats 14
Tugs at Play 16
    Glossary . . . . Inside back cover
    Index . . . . Inside back cover

Ellen Ungaro

The Busy Port

Ships travel all the way across the Pacific Ocean to reach these **ports**.

San Francisco, California

How do these giant ships make their way through a **harbor's** narrow **channels** and crowded waters?

Seattle, Washington

Tugboats help them! It's a tugboat's job to move these **cargo ships** safely in and out of the harbor.

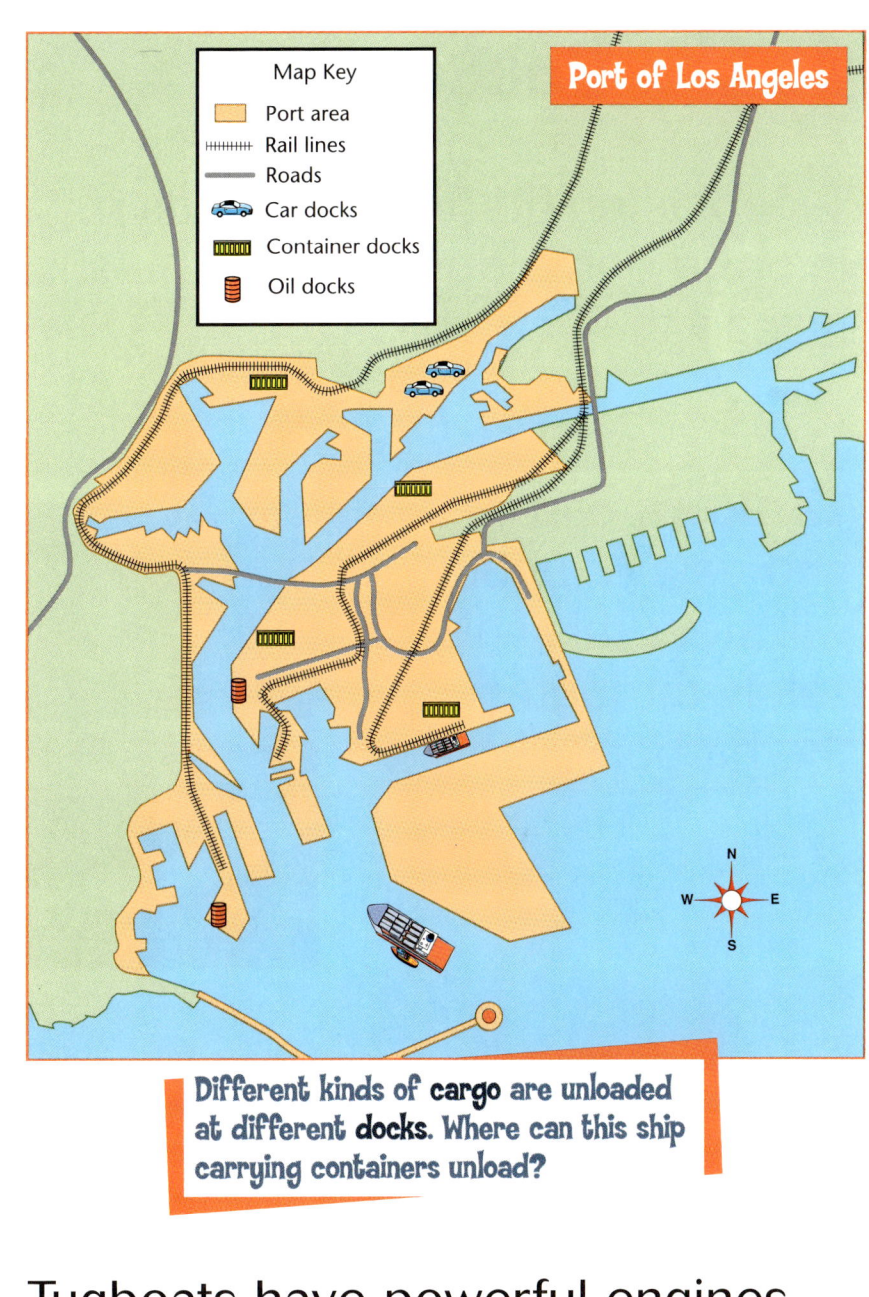

Map Key
- Port area
- Rail lines
- Roads
- Car docks
- Container docks
- Oil docks

Port of Los Angeles

Different kinds of **cargo** are unloaded at different **docks**. Where can this ship carrying containers unload?

Tugboats have powerful engines that help them push or pull boats that are many times their size.

5

At the Dock

Tugboats guide different kinds of cargo ships into the port's docks. Then the ships can unload their cargo.

Tankers carry oil and gas. A tugboat will steer this ship safely through the harbor.

Some ships carry cars. After the tugboat helps the ship into the dock, workers can drive the cars right off the ship.

Can you see how tugboats push this **container ship** up to the dock?

Each of the containers on this ship holds something different. There may be clothing, computers, or toys inside.

The containers are loaded onto trains or trucks and delivered to **warehouses** and stores.

Then the ship is loaded with new containers, and a tugboat leads it back out to sea.

Traveling on the River Road

A towboat is another kind of tugboat. Towboats work on the Mississippi River.

How many barges is this towboat pushing?

Towboats push **barges** up and down the Mississippi River. These long flat boats are filled with coal, steel, lumber, grain, or other large cargo.

This barge is being filled with corn.

The towboat's captain must steer this fleet of barges safely up the river.

Port
Power Plant

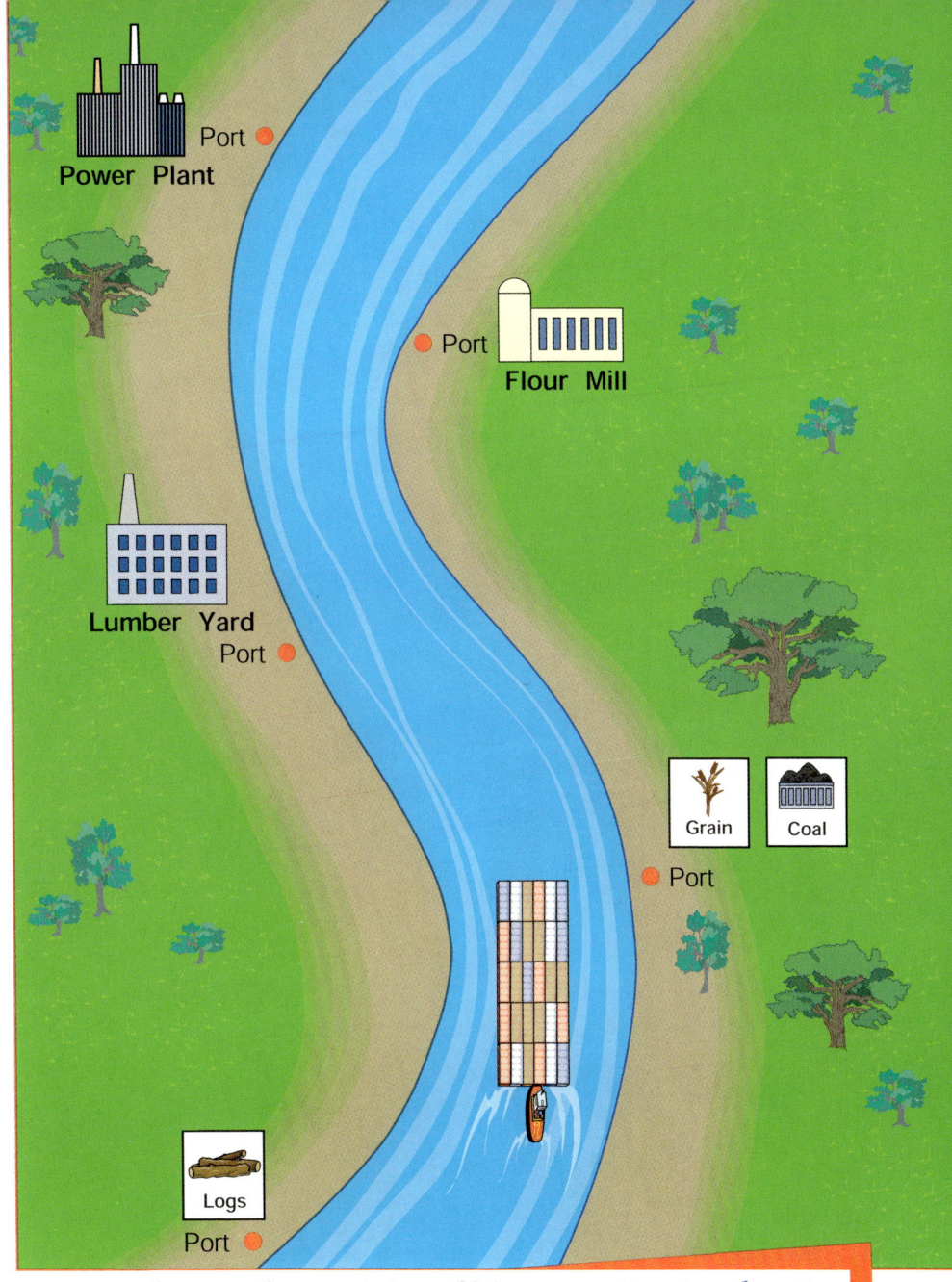

Port
Flour Mill

Lumber Yard
Port

Grain   Coal

Port

Logs
Port

> Towboats pick up and drop off barges as they travel on the river. A towboat picks up barges of coal, logs, and grain at different river ports. Where do you think the towboat might drop off each of these barges?

13

Tugs: The Working Boats

Tugboats are called working boats. They do many different jobs in harbors, on the ocean, on rivers, and on lakes.

Some tugs tow ships that have broken down into port.

Some tugs break the ice on lakes so ships can pass through.

Some tugs help move things that can't fit on a truck. These tugs are moving part of a tunnel.

Tugs at Play

A tugboat's **crew** works hard to keep things moving on the river or in the harbor. At the tugboat races in Detroit, Michigan, the crews have a chance to play!